MACDONALD FIRST LIBRARY

Weather

Macdonald Educational
49-50 Poland Street
London W1

There is air all around the earth.
This layer of air is called the atmosphere.
If we looked at the earth from space, we
should see the atmosphere as a blue haze.
We should not see a haze around the moon.
The moon has no atmosphere.

The atmosphere is very important.
It gives us the air we breathe.
It protects us from the strongest heat of
the sun during the day.
And it keeps the earth warm at night, like
a blanket.

Sometimes the air is warm; sometimes it is cold.
Sometimes the air is damp; sometimes it is dry.
These are some of the changes we call weather.

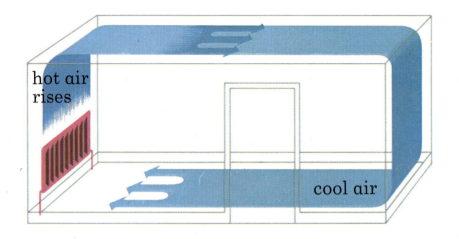

hot air
rises

cool air

If you hold your hands over a radiator, you
can feel hot air rising.

The air is made hot by the radiator.

The hot air expands and rises because it is
lighter than the cold air around it.

As the hot air rises, cooler air moves in to
take its place.

The same sort of thing happens in the
atmosphere.

4

Heat from the sun warms the land on the Equator.

The land heats the air above it.

The heated air rises.

As it rises it cools.

Finally the cool air sinks and spreads over the surface.

We call these movements of air wind.

cooler
air

sun's heat

hot
air

Equator

cooler
air

force 1

force 2

force 3

A wind may be light or it may be strong.
Weathermen use a scale to describe the speed,
or force, of winds.
The pictures show how this scale works.
The scale number goes up as the wind gets
stronger.

force 7

force 8

force 9

force 4

force 5

force 6

At Force 1 the wind is moving at only a few
miles an hour.
You can hardly feel it.
But in a Force 10 gale the wind may be
travelling at over 60 miles per hour.
It can blow down trees and damage houses.

force 10

force 11

force 12

The atmosphere also
holds water.
The water is in the form
of vapour.
When water is heated, it
slowly disappears.
The heat makes the water
change into vapour.
It disappears into the
atmosphere.
This is called evaporation.

Evaporation happens all
the time.
The sun heats the water
in rivers and lakes and
the water evaporates
into the air.

8

evaporation

condensation

dew

Warm air holds more water vapour than cold air.
When warm air gets colder, some of the
vapour turns back into water.
This is called condensation.
If a glass of iced water is put in a warm
room, water will condense on the cold glass.
Dew is condensed water.
It comes from air which has cooled at night.

land fog

Condensation also causes fog.
Fog forms when warm, moist air near the
ground is cooled.
The water vapour condenses into millions
of tiny drops of water.
This is called fog.
Fogs often form on clear, cold nights.
The land cools very quickly and the air
above it gets cold.
This makes water vapour condense as fog.

Fogs form at sea, too.
They often form when a stream of cold sea
water meets warmer water.
The air moving over the warm water is warm
and moist.
When this air passes over the cold stream,
it is quickly cooled.
Its water vapour condenses and fog forms.

sea fog

cirrus

cirro-stratus

cirro-cumulus

alto-stratus

nimbo-stratus

stratus

Condensation also happens in the sky.
It makes clouds.
Clouds are millions of tiny water droplets.

If it is very cold, the clouds are made of
ice crystals not water droplets.

There are many different kinds of clouds.

12

alto-cumulus

strato-cumulus

cumulus

cumulo-nimbus

Some look like grey blankets across the sky.
These are called stratus clouds.
Cirrus clouds are little wisps, high in the sky.
They are made of ice crystals.
Cumulus clouds look like puffs of cotton wool.
Some cumulus clouds grow into big, dark
thunderclouds.
They are called cumulo-nimbus clouds.

water droplets

Clouds are made of tiny water droplets.
The droplets are so small and light that they stay up in the air.

drops grow bigger

The droplets are always moving.
When they bump into each other they join together and grow larger.

rain falls

They become heavy.
They may become too heavy to hang in the air.
Then they fall to the ground as rain.

14

Clouds and rain are caused when air rises
and cools.
Sometimes moving air is forced to rise over
high land.
The air cools as it rises.
The higher it rises, the cooler it becomes.
The cooler it becomes, the more vapour
condenses.
The droplets grow bigger and bigger and fall
as rain.
This is why it rains a lot in the mountains.

cloud

air rises

ea

snow crystals

Sometimes the water
droplets in clouds are
frozen.
The tiny ice crystals may
get bigger and heavier
because droplets freeze
around them.
They may become so heavy
that they start to fall.
If the air below is very
cold, the crystals fall
as snow.
If the air is warm, they
melt and fall as rain.

frost

Snow crystals always have six sides.
But each is a different pattern.

Frost makes beautiful patterns, too.
You can see the patterns on the window on a
frosty night.
Frost is caused by vapour condensing on a
very cold surface.

warm front

warm air

cold air

Great masses of warm air and cold air move
through the atmosphere all the time.
Where a mass of warm air meets a mass of
cold air the weather changes.
The line where the two masses meet is called
a front.

When a mass of warm air overtakes a mass of
cold air there is a warm front.

The warm air is lighter than the cold air.
It rises slowly over the cold air.
As it rises clouds form and rain falls.

When cold air overtakes a mass of warm air
there is a cold front.
The cold air burrows under the warm air and
pushes it up.
Clouds form and often heavy rain falls.
There may even be thunderstorms.

Thunderstorms happen when hot, moist air rises fast and cools quickly.
Dark clouds form and big drops of rain or hail fall.
Lightning flashes and thunder crashes.
Lightning is an electric spark.
Thunder is the noise caused by lightning as it travels to the ground.

Hail forms when a rain-
drop goes up and down
through a thundercloud.
As it goes up it freezes.
As it comes down it picks
up a layer of water.
This goes on until it is
so heavy that it falls.

hailstone
cut in half

Hurricanes are violent storms.
They begin over warm seas, where the air is hot and moist.
The air circles round and round as it rises.
It goes faster and faster and faster.
Soon the wind is roaring and the rain is beating down.
Hurricanes cause a lot of damage when they reach the land.

hurricane

The centre, or 'eye', of a hurricane is very calm.

Hurricanes can be tracked by aircraft or on radar screens, and they can be photographed by satellites travelling around Earth. Weathermen can warn people when one is coming.

radar screen

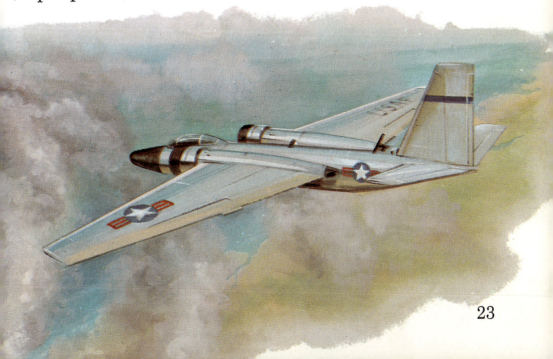

23

A tornado is another
kind of violent storm.
It is a great column
of whirling air.
It reaches from the
ground right up to the
clouds.
Tornadoes are very
dangerous.

tornado

Tornadoes begin over very hot land.
Cold air flows in and the hot air rises very
fast and whirls round and round.
As the tornado moves it sucks up anything
in its path.
Dust, fences, roofs and even cars are lifted
high into the air and dropped back to earth.
Luckily, tornadoes do not last very long.

Our weather changes from day to day.
But the kind of weather we have from year
to year stays the same.
This is called the climate.
Different parts of the world have different
climates.
Some are hot; some are cold.
Some are wet; some are dry.
The sun is hottest at the equator.
Lands near the equator are hot all the time.
Near the north and south poles it is very
cold all the time.
Between the equator and the poles, lands
have warm, or hot, summers and cool, or cold,
winters.
In the wettest lands it rains every day.
In the driest lands it may not rain for many
years.

north pole

equator

south pole

27

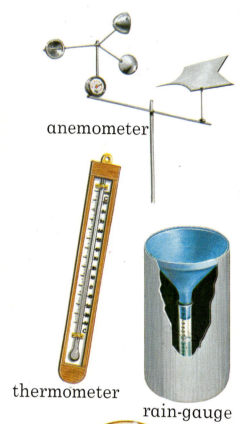

anemometer

thermometer

rain-gauge

barometer

Many kinds of instruments are used to 'measure' the weather.

A thermometer is used to measure how hot or cold the air is.

A barometer is used to measure the pressure of the air.

An anemometer is used to measure the speed of the wind.

It has cups which catch the wind and spin round. The stronger the wind, the faster the cups spin round.

Rainfall is measured with
a rain-gauge.
The rain falls into a
funnel and drips into
a tube.
The amount of water in
the tube shows how much
rain has fallen.

We can find out about
the weather high in the
sky with radio-sondes.
These are instruments
which are carried by
balloons, filled with gas.
The instruments send
back information to the
earth.

radio-sonde

satellite

Men who study the weather are called meteorologists.
A meteorologist tries to tell us what the weather will be like.
He 'forecasts' the weather.

tracking station

He uses weather instruments to help him.
He also finds out what the weather is like at other weather stations.

photograph

He may even use pictures of the clouds taken by weather satellites high above the earth.

Meteorologists make charts to show what the
weather is like.
They use special symbols to show rain, fog,
cold fronts, warm fronts, and the speed of
the wind.
There is a symbol for every kind of weather.
By looking at the chart, the meteorologist
can forecast what the weather will be like
for the next day.
And he is usually right.

weather chart

Index

Anemometer, 28
Atmosphere, 2
Barometer, 28
Climate, 26, 27
Clouds, 13, 21
Condensation, 9
Dew, 9
Evaporation, 8
Fog, 10, 11
Forecasting, 30, 31
Fronts, 18, 19
Frost, 17

Hail, 21
Hurricane, 22, 23
Meteorologist, 30, 31
Radio-sonde, 29
Rain, 14, 15
Rain-gauge, 28, 29
Snow, 16
Thermometer, 28
Thunderstorm, 20, 21
Tornado, 24, 25
Weather satellite, 30
Wind, 5-7

MACDONALD FIRST LIBRARY

1 Prehistoric Animals
2 The Airline Pilot
3 Into Space
4 Knights and Castles
5 The Postman
6 Insects That Live Together
7 By the Sea
8 How Flowers Live
9 Water
10 Number
11 Space
12 Sounds and Music
13 Cats
14 Frogs and Toads
15 Mushrooms and Toadstools
16 The Policeman
17 Under the Sea
18 Ships of Long Ago
19 Air
20 Cold Lands
21 Spiders
22 Pirates and Buccaneers
23 Size
24 Fire
25 Weather
26 Deserts
27 Skyscrapers
28 Monkeys and Apes
29 Trains and Railways
30 Trees and Wood
31 Cowboys
32 Time and Clocks
33 Light and Colour
34 Birds and Migration
35 The Universe

36 Farms and Farmers
37 Rocks and Mining
38 Rivers and River Life
39 Snakes and Lizards
40 Roads and Motorways
41 Ports and Harbours
42 Bridges and Tunnels
43 Towns and Cities
44 Horses and Ponies
45 Aeroplanes and Balloons
46 The Story of Cars
47 Mountains
48 Electricity
49 Television
50 Photography
51 The Jungle
52 The Dog Family
53 Gypsies and Nomads
54 Ballet and Dance
55 Paper and Printing
56 Food and Drink
57 Cloth and Weaving
58 Lakes and Dams
59 Building
60 Butterflies and Moths
61 Vanishing Animals
62 Animals that Burrow
63 Fuel and Energy
64 Animals with Shells
65 The Theatre
66 Health and Disease
67 Pollution
68 The Cinema
69 Signals and Messages
70 Fishing

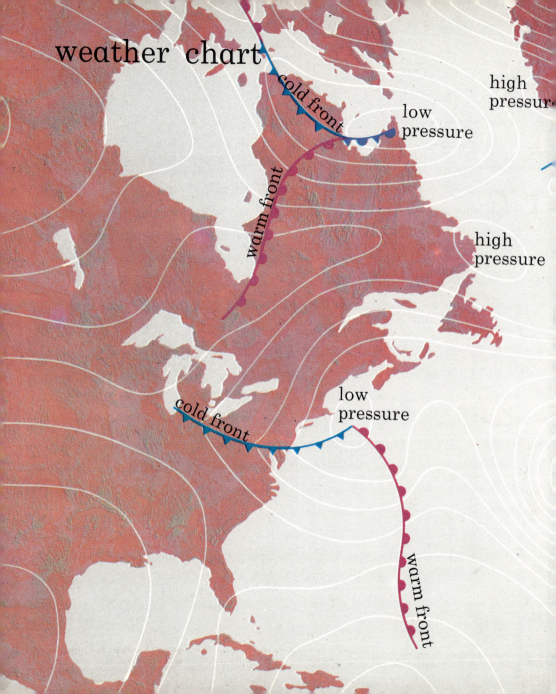

weather chart

cold front

low
pressure

high
pressur

warm front

high
pressure

cold front

low
pressure

warm front